VALUE INVEST

I0036014

THE BUFFETT TECHNIQUES OF ACCUMULATING WEALTH WITH PRACTICAL STRATEGIES TO ALWAYS CHOOSE THE INTELLIGENT INVESTMENT

Descrierea CIP a Bibliotecii Naționale a României

Value Investing. The Buffett Techniques Of Accumulating Wealth With Practical Strategies To Always Choose The Intelligent Investment. – Bucharest: My Ebook Publishing House, 2018
ISBN 978-606-983-628-6

VALUE INVESTING

THE BUFFETT TECHNIQUES OF ACCUMULATING WEALTH WITH PRACTICAL STRATEGIES TO ALWAYS CHOOSE THE INTELLIGENT INVESTMENT

My Ebook Publishing House
Bucharest, 2018

CONTENTS

INTRODUCTION

*I want to use this means to thank and congratulate you for downloading this book "**Value Investing: The Buffett Techniques Of Accumulating Wealth With Practical Strategies To Always Choose The Intelligent Investment**"*

Value investors like Warren Buffett can beat the stock market, as well as most other cash supervisors too. Why? What do value investors do another way for different investors? What's more, if value investing works so well, for what reason do as a such couple of individuals utilize it?

In this book, we will take in the basics of examination, projection, valuation, and execution. We will initially figure out how to break down organizations' authentic implementation by computing basic measurements like profit for invested capital. Second, we will find how to extend future corporate implementation utilizing structures. Again, we will master how to value a stock, and lastly, we will figure out how to actualize a valued technique by avoiding here and now revealing, predispositions, and different obstacles. By handling the instruments of value investing and the keys to their usage, understudies will pick up knowledge into the capital management system that performs best finished the ordeal.

Thanks again for downloading this book and I hope you enjoy it.

Copyright 2018 by Zen Mastery - All rights reserved.

This document is geared towards providing exact and reliable information in regards to the topic and issue covered. The publication is sold with the idea that the publisher is not required to render accounting, officially permitted, or otherwise, qualified services. If advice is necessary, legal or professional, a practiced individual in the profession should be ordered.

- From a Declaration of Principles which was accepted and approved equally by a Committee of the American Bar Association and a Committee of Publishers and Associations.

In no way is it legal to reproduce, duplicate, or transmit any part of this document in either electronic means or in printed format. Recording of this publication is strictly prohibited and any storage of this document is not allowed unless with written permission from the publisher. All rights reserved.

The information provided herein is stated to be truthful and consistent, in that any liability, in terms of inattention or otherwise, by any usage or abuse of any policies, processes, or directions contained within is the solitary and utter responsibility of the recipient reader. Under no circumstances will any legal responsibility or blame be held against the publisher for any reparation, damages, or monetary loss due to the information herein, either directly or indirectly.

Respective authors own all copyrights not held by the publisher.

The information herein is offered for informational purposes solely, and is universal as so. The presentation of the information is without contract or any type of guarantee assurance.

The trademarks that are used are without any consent, and the publication of the trademark is without permission or backing by the trademark owner. All trademarks and brands within this book are for clarifying purposes only and are the owned by the owners themselves, not affiliated with this document.

CHAPTER ONE

UNDERSTANDING WHAT VALUE INVESTING IS?

Value investing is an investment system where stocks that are chosen for trade are not as much as their inherent values. Value investors effectively look for stocks they trust the market has undervalued. Investors who utilize this technique trust the market blows up to significant and awful news, bringing about stock value developments that don't compare with an organization's long-haul basics, giving a chance to profit when the cost is flattened.

Undervalued stocks come to fruition through investor silliness. Regularly, value investors try to profit off this unreasonableness by choosing stocks with lower-than-normal, cost to-book proportions, lower-than-normal cost to-income proportions as well as higher profit yields. These numbers are contrasted with an organization's characteristic value, after which, a value investor invests if the similar cost is sufficiently high.

Nonetheless, there is an issue with value investing in that evaluating the characteristic value of a stock is troublesome. Two investors can be given precisely the same and place an alternate value on an organization. Thus, another focal concept of value investing is that of "edge of security." Value investors need to purchase an amount at a sufficiently significant rebate to permit some space for the mistake in the estimation of value.

Shouldn't we as a whole be value investors? Who needs to purchase terrible stocks? In any case, for this situation, value investing alludes to a specific theory that drives the way an investor approaches choosing stocks.

12

Value investing isn't shopping the deal receptacle for a considerable length of time and ended models. It isn't tied in with purchasing anything under of about $3 per share.

Value investing is tied in with discovering stocks that the market has not accurately evaluated. As such, a stock that is worth more than is reflected in the present cost.

Moreover, value investing is subjective. Some value investors just take a gander at startup resources and income and don't put any value on future development. Other value investors base their systems entirely around the estimation of future development and money streams. In spite of the distinctive philosophies, the fundamental rationale is a value investor should purchase something for short of what he supposes it is as of now worth.

Value investing is an investment worldview which for the most part includes purchasing bonds that show up underpriced by some sort of urgent investigation.

However, it has taken numerous structures since its commencement. It gets from the thoughts on investment that Benjamin Graham and David Dodd started instructing at Columbia Business college in 1928 and consequently created in their 1934 content Security Examination. As illustrations, such securities might be stock out in the open organizations that trade at rebates to book value or substantial book value, have high-profit yields, have low-cost to-procuring products or have low-cost to-book proportions.

Prominent advocates of value investing, including Berkshire Hathaway executive Warren Buffett, have contended that the pith of value investing is purchasing stocks at not precisely their inherent value. The markdown of the market cost to the inherent value is the thing that Benjamin Graham called the "edge of wellbeing." The characteristic value is the marked down value of all future distributions. Be that as it may, the future dissemination and the suitable rebate rate must be suppositions. Graham never prescribed utilizing future numbers, just past ones). Throughout the previous 25 years, Warren Buffett has taken the value investing concept significantly encourage with an emphasis on "finding an extraordinary organization at a sensible cost" instead of bland organizations at a deal price.

Graham never utilized the expression, "value investing" — the term was begotten later to help depict his thoughts and has brought about the colossal distortion of his standards, the chief being that Graham essentially suggested shabby stocks.

However, it wouldn't be out of place to know who a real Value Investor is and defines a value Investor?

The value investor, maybe more than some other sort of investor, is more worried about the business and its basics than different impacts on the stock's cost.

Basics, for example, income development, profits, income, and book value are more vital than market factors on the stock's cost. Value investors likewise purchase and hold investors who are with an organization as long as possible.

If the basics are sound, yet the stock's cost is underneath its outstanding value, the value investor knows this is a probable investment hopeful. The market has inaccurately valued the stock. At the point when the market remedies that error, the stock's cost should encounter a pleasant ascent.

Is it a contender for a value investor? Perhaps, however likely not. Value investors aren't usually inspired by whipped stocks unless there is no significant explanation for the drop in cost.

The Market's Right

This happens. Most of the time, the market is right, and a stock gets pounded given any number of principal sound reasons (declining profit, declining incomes, are great illustrations) or something critical changes in their market or product offering.

Undervalued stocks occur through investor mindlessness. Commonly, value investors try to profit off this silliness by choosing stocks with lower-than-normal cost to-book proportions, lower-than-normal cost to-income proportions or potentially higher profit yields. These numbers are contrasted with an organization's intrinsic value, after which, a value investor invests if the near value is sufficiently high.

Nonetheless, there is an issue with value investing in that evaluating the natural value of a stock is troublesome. Two investors can be given precisely the same and place an alternate value on an organization. Thus, another focal concept of value investing is that of "edge of security." Value investors need to purchase an amount at a sufficiently significant markdown to permit some space for the mistake in the estimation of value.

Also, value investing is subjective. Some value investors just take a gander at display resources and profit and don't put any value on future development. Other value investors base their methodologies entirely around the estimation of future development and money streams. In spite of the distinctive philosophies, the primary rationale is a value investor should purchase something for short of what he supposes it is as of now worth.

CHAPTER TWO

THE ECONOMICS OF VALUE INVESTING

Over the years, the markets have changed, so too has value investing. Throughout the years, Graham's unique value investing technique has been adjusted, balanced, and reexamined in an assortment of courses by investors and market investigators expecting to enhance how well a value investing approach performs for investors. Indeed, even Graham himself concocted additional measurements and definitions went for all the more precisely deciding the excellent value of a stock.

What's more, excellent stock investigation requires that you audit past and current financial measurements with an eye to the future, anticipating how well you figure an organization will charge pushing ahead, given its present funds, resources, liabilities, marketplace position, and plans for development.

It's likewise imperative to abstain from losing all sense of direction in a merely numerical investigation to the point where you dismiss the backwoods for the trees. Non-numerical "value" factors that investors ought not to ignore incorporate things, for example, how adequately an organization's management is accomplishing objectives, advancing the organization in a way that is reliable with seeking after its corporate statement of purpose. An organization might indicate high productivity for the occasion, yet in the present too much-focused marketplace, an organization that isn't painstakingly mapping, arranging out, and looking into (and when required, re-directing) it's encouraging will almost dependably, in the long run, be obscured by an organization that is doing those things.

As an investor, it's imperative to remember that there's more than one savvy approach to profit in the stock market. It is also essential that an intending investor is enthusiastic about wage investing while looking for an investment methodology, it's best to be educated about the potential dangers of and contrasts between each approach. Here we will center around growth and value investing, two necessary procedures to perceive in stock investing.

Both of these market systems look to give the ideal returns, so the factual distinction between the two is in their approach.

Before then, let us quickly understand what is growth investing and what it is all about?

Growth investing is a style of investment methodology concentrated on capital appreciation. Those who take after this style, known as growth investors, invest in organizations that display indications of better than expected growth, regardless of whether the share cost seems costly as far as measurements, for example, cost to-profit or cost to-book ratios. In the run of the mill use, the expression "growth investing" appears differently about the procedure known as value investing.

Notwithstanding, some outstanding investors, for example, Warren Buffett have expressed that there is no hypothetical contrast between the ideas of value and ("Growth and Value Investing are joined at the hip"), as growth is dependably a part in the figuring of cost, constituting a variable whose significance can go from unimportant to tremendous and whose effect can be detrimental and additionally positive.

In tempestuous markets, growth investors can see wild instabilities in their portfolios, particularly contrasted with value investors who tend to purchase stocks of organizations that are moderately reasonable or undervalued.

Indeed, even with that unpredictability, numerous investors may, in any case, need to investigate the "growth" situation. In light of that, there are various alternatives to take a peek at.

Differentiated High Growth Stocks

High-growth shared funds and exchange-traded funds (ETFs) possess large amounts of the values market. These funds regularly involve an arrangement of stocks with high growth measurements in LOLreakey regions of the organization's financial execution, including income, profit, and income. They additionally have elevated valuation measures, for example, a high-cost to-profit (P/E) proportion.

Investors can buy enhanced, high-growth index funds that look to coordinate the risk and return of an index of high-growth stocks. Then again, they can efficiently pick oversaw high-growth funds. Given the differing attributes of high-growth stocks and the quick moving nature of the monetary cycle, a few investors incline toward managed efficiently funds and the vigilant gaze of a store administrator that accompanies them. American Funds is a primary growth subsidize director with various high-performing growth funds.

Singular High-Growth Stocks

Investors equipped for risking on abnormal amounts of risk can likewise invest in different growth stocks. These stocks can be found overall market areas. Utilizing significant examination, tenacious investors can recognize the most promising growth stocks in the market at a given time. Measurements, for example, substantial income, profit growth, and a high P/E proportion assign stocks with high growth potential.

Broadened Small-Cap Stocks

Investors regularly look to little top stocks as driving growth investments because the lion's share of this market section highlights developing organizations new to market exchanges. Index funds and efficiently oversaw funds concentrated on high-growth little top stocks offer the shot for market-beating returns.

Focused High-Growth Stocks

High growth describes various market parts and focused market subsets. These portions offer huge come back to investors who recognize them early. One such case in 2016 is the market for distributed computing. Distributed computing incomes have been developing significantly, with high-performing organizations in this market classification speaking to a LOlaide to investors.

CHAPTER THREE

GROWTH VERSUS VALUE INVESTING

Before we advance to audit universal value investing and afterward take a gander at a portion of the more up to date, elective value investing systems, it's critical to take note of that "value investing" and "growth investing" are not two opposing or fundamentally unrelated ways to deal with picking stocks. The fundamental thought of value investing – choosing as of now undervalued stocks that you hope to increment in value later on – is undoubtedly centered around expected growth.

The contrasts between value investing and growth investing techniques have a tendency to be all the more merely a question of stressing several financial measurements (and to some degree a distinction in risk resistance, with growth investors commonly ready to acknowledge more copious amounts of risk). At last, value investing, growth investing, or some other essential stock assessment approach has a similar real objective: picking stocks that will give an investor the ideal degree of profitability.

At some point prior, Graham proposed and clarified a technique for screening stocks that he created to help even the most unpracticed investors with their stock portfolio determinations. That is one of the real interests of Graham's value investing approach – the way that it's not excessively mind-boggling or muddled, and can, in this way, be used efficiently by the reasonable investor.

Likewise, with an investing system, Graham's value investing procedure includes some fundamental ideas that underlie or shape the establishment or reason for the technique. For Graham, the underlying concept was that of characteristic value – notably, the inherent value of an organization or its stock. The pith of value investing is utilizing a stock investigation technique to decide the stock's original value, with an eye toward purchasing stocks whose present share cost is beneath its honest to goodness value or worth.

Value investors are applying the same rationale from cautious customers, is hoping to recognize stocks that are "a great purchase," that are offering at a cost lower than the absolute value they speak to. A value investor looks out and gobbles up what they decide are undervalued stocks, with the conviction that the market will in the long run "adjust" the share cost to a more elevated amount that all the more precisely speaks to its actual value.

Graham's way to deal with value investing was intended for building up a necessary procedure for stock screening that the reasonable investor could without much of a stretch use. He managed to keep things genuinely essential, however then again, typical value investing is somewhat more required than simply the regularly discussed hold back of, "Purchase stocks with a cost to-book (P/B) proportion of under 1.0."

The P/B proportion rule for distinguishing undervalued stocks is, indeed, just a single of various criteria which Graham used to enable him to recognize undervalued stocks. There's some contention among value investing devotees with respect to whether one should utilize a 10-point criteria agenda that Graham made, a more extended 17-point plan, a refining of both of the criteria records that usually shows up as a four-or five-point agenda, or either of a few single standard stock determination strategies that Graham additionally pushed.

While trying to maintain a strategic distance from however much disarray as could be expected, we will exhibit here the fundamental criteria that Graham himself considered most imperative in distinguishing great value stocks, i.e., those with a characteristic value more noteworthy than their market cost.

- A value stock ought to have P/B proportion of 1.0 or lower; the P/B proportion is critical because it speaks to an examination of the share cost of an organization's benefits. One noteworthy confinement of the P/B proportion is that it capacities best when used to survey capital-serious organizations, however, is less successful when connected to non-capital-concentrated firms.

Note: Rather than searching for an outright P/B proportion lower than 1.0, investors may just search for organizations with a P/B proportion that is lower than the standard P/B proportion of similar organizations in its industry or market area.

- The cost to-profit (P/E) proportion ought to be under 40% of the stock's most elevated P/E over the past five years.

• Look at a share cost that is under 67% (66%) of the unmistakable per share book value, AND under 67% of the organization's net current resource value (NCAV).

Note: The share-cost to-NCAV standard is now and again utilized as an independent instrument for recognizing undervalued stocks. Graham considered an organization's NCAV to be a standout amongst the most accurate portrayals of an organization's actual characteristic value.

• An organization's aggregate book value ought to be more prominent than its aggregate obligation.

Note: A related, or maybe an option, financial metric to this is analyzing the fundamental obligation proportion – the present proportion – which ought to, in any event, is more prominent than 1.0 and ideally higher than 2.0.

• An organization's aggregate obligation ought not to surpass double the NCAV, and aggregate current liabilities and long-haul duty ought not to be more noteworthy than the company's total stockholder value.

Investors can try different things by utilizing Graham's different criteria and decide for themselves which of the valuation measurements or rules they consider to be fundamental and dependable. There are a few investors who still utilize just an examination of a stock's P/B proportion to decide if a stock is undervalued. Others depend intensely, if not solely, on different current share cost with the organization's NCAV. More mindful, moderate investors may just purchase stocks that pass each one of Graham's recommended screening tests.

Elective Methods of Determining Value

Value investors keep on giving Graham and his value investing measurements consideration. In any case, the improvement of new points from which to figure and survey profit implies that elective techniques for distinguishing underpriced stocks have emerged too.

One expanding important value metric is the Discounted Cash Flow (DCF) recipe.

DCF and Reverse DCF Valuation

Numerous accountants and other financial experts have turned out to be enthusiastic devotees of DCF examination. DCF is one of only a handful couple of financial measurements that consider the time value of cash – the idea that cash accessible now is more important than a similar measure of money obtainable sooner or later because whatever money is available now can be invested and accordingly used to create more liquidity.

DCF examination utilizes future free income (FCF) projections and markdown rates that are computed using the Weighted Average Cost of Capital (WACC) to appraise the present value of an organization, with the underlying thought being that its inherent value is to a great extent subject to the organization's capacity to produce income.

The fundamental computation of a DCF investigation is as per the following:

Reasonable Value = The organization's Attempt value – the organization's obligation

(Attempt value is an elective metric to market capitalization value. It speaks to market capitalization + commitment + favored shares – add up to money, including money reciprocals).

DCF investigation is especially appropriate for assessing organizations that have stable, generally unsurprising money streams since the essential shortcoming of DCF examination is that it relies upon accurate appraisals of future money streams.

A few experts like to apply the turn around DCF investigation to conquer the vulnerability of future income projections. Turn around DCF examination begins with a known amount – the present share value – and after that figures the money streams that would be required to create that current valuation. Once the required income is resolved, at that point assessing the organization's stock as undervalued or overvalued is as essential as making a judgment about how sensible (or preposterous) it is to anticipate that the organization will have the capacity to produce the required measure of money streams essential to maintain or propel the present share cost.

An undervalued stock is distinguished when an expert verifies that an organization can undoubtedly create and maintain all that anyone could need income to legitimize the present share cost.

New Price-Earnings Ratio

Katsenelson's Absolute P/E Model

Katsenelson's model, created by Vitally Katsenelson, is another elective value investing investigation instrument that is considered especially perfect for assessing organizations that have unequivocally positive, settled profit scores. The Katsenelson show centers around giving investors a more solid P/E proportion, known as "supreme P/E."

The model modifies the current P/E proportion as per a few factors, for example, income growth, profit yield, and profit consistency. The equation is as per the following:

Supreme PE = (Earnings Growth Points + Dividend Points) x [1 + (1 – Business Risk)] x [1 + (1 – Financial Risk)] x [1 + (1 – Earnings Visibility)]

Profit growth focuses are controlled by beginning with a no-growth P/E value of 8, and afterward including .65 focuses for each 100 premise focuses the anticipated growth rate increments until the point when you achieve 16%. Over 16%, .5 focuses are included for each 100 premise focuses on anticipated growth.

The total P/E number delivered is then contrasted with the customary P/E number.

If the whole P/E number is higher than the standard P/E proportion, at that point that demonstrates the stock is undervalued. The bigger the inconsistency between the total P/E and the standard P/E, the better a deal the stock is. For instance, if a stock's outright P/E is 20 while the usual P/E proportion is just 11, at that point the genuine inherent value of the stock is likely substantially higher than the present share cost, as the supreme P/E number shows that investors are presumably ready to pay significantly more for the organization's current income.

Ben Graham Number

You don't need to turn away from Ben Graham to locate an elective value investing metric. Graham himself made another value evaluation equation that investors may utilize – the Ben Graham Number.

The recipe for ascertaining the Ben Graham Number is as per the following:

Ben Graham Number = the square base of [22.5 x (Earnings per share (EPS)) x (Book value per share)]

For instance, the Ben Graham Number for a stock with an EPS of $1.50 and a book value of $10 per share computes out to $18.37.

Graham, for the most part, felt that an organization's P/E proportion shouldn't be higher than 15 and that its cost to-book (P/B) proportion shouldn't surpass 1.5. That is the place the 22.5 in the equation is gotten from (15 x 1.5 = 22.5). In any case, with the valuation levels that are ordinary nowadays, the most extreme reasonable P/E may be moved to around 25.

Once you've computed a stock's Ben Graham Number – which is intended to speak to the actual per-share characteristic value of the organization – you at that point contrast it with the stock's present share cost.

On the off chance that the present share cost is lower than the Ben Graham Number, this demonstrates the stock is undervalued and might be considered as a purchase.

Value investors are continually hoping to purchase undervalued stocks at a rebate to influence benefits with negligible to chance. There is an assortment of apparatuses and methodologies that investors can use to Attempt to decide the absolute value of a stock and regardless of whether it's a solid match for their investment portfolio.

The best stock valuation process is never only a mathematical equation that one attachments numbers into and after that consequently get a firm, ensured assurance of a specific stock as a "decent" or "awful" investment. While there are vital stock valuation equations and financial measurements to consider, the way toward assessing a stock as a potential expansion of your investment portfolio is at last part artistry and part science.

CHAPTER FOUR

VALUE INVESTING STRATEGY

For most investors, the superlative way to deal with value ownership is a valid currency cost averaging program setup, with profits, reinvested, into ease, comprehensively enhanced index finance following something, for example. A couple of investors, regularly fruitful entrepreneurs, officials, or scholastics, like to choose singular securities, assembling a portfolio step by determined step in light of an investigation of the individual firms.

The Strategies

For those few do-it-without anyone's help investors, who are regularly called dynamic investors, venturesome investors, or forceful investors - the father of value investing himself, Benjamin Graham, recognized five classifications of basic stock investing that could bring about palatable or more than attractive returns. For a drew in portfolio director who needed to compound capital, he illuminated these in his 1949 version of The Intelligent Investor:

Deal Purchases - Selecting issues which are offering significantly beneath their actual value, as estimated by sensibly tried and true systems

Specific Trading - Picking out points which, over a time of a year or less, will improve the situation in the market than the regular stock

General Trading - Anticipating or partaking in the moves of the market all in all, as reflected in the well-known "midpoints

Purchasing Cheap and Selling Dear - Coming into the market when costs and estimation are discouraged and offering out when both are commended

Long-Pull Selection - Picking out organizations which will succeed throughout the years significantly more than the normal venture. (These are regularly alluded to as "growth stocks.")

Graham goes ahead to address the particular bind each dynamic investor will look in deciding how to deal with his or her portfolio saying, "Regardless of whether the investor should endeavor to purchase low and offer high, or whether he ought to be substance to hold sound securities through various challenges - subject just too intermittent examination of their inherent benefits - is one of the few decisions of strategy which the individual must make for himself.

Here demeanor and individual circumstance may well be the deciding variables. A man near business undertakings, who is in the propensity for framing judgments with regards to the financial standpoint and of following up on them, will typically be slanted to make comparable conclusions about the general level of stock costs. It would be coherent for such investors to be pulled in to the purchase low-offer high system. In any case, proficient men and affluent individuals not dynamic in business would more be able to vaccinate their reasoning from the impact of year-to-year vacillations effectively. For this gathering, the more alluring decision might be the less difficult one of purchasing painstakingly when funds are accessible and laying the mean weight on the salary return throughout the years."

Each approach requires a reasonable, taught, precise application. The key is *consistency*. It fits pleasantly with most people inclinations and values; like perceptive long-haul, around a couple of enormous thoughts as we sometimes prefer not to be adhered to our work area, watching what the stock market does on any given day or week.

In this specific region of portfolio management, there is no correct answer as long as you are carrying on judiciously, utilizing actualities and information to move down your practices, and always endeavoring to diminish risk, while keeping up liquidity and the wellbeing. You need to choose for yourself which sort of investor you will be.

CHAPTER FIVE

CRITICISM OF VALUE INVESTING

Value stocks don't beat growth stocks, as shown in the late 1990s. Also, when value stocks perform well, it may not imply that the market is wasteful. However, it might suggest that value stocks are intrinsically less secure and in this manner require more noteworthy returns.

One of the focal elements of investors in a market economy is to guide cash-flow to its most productive use. This fixation in Value Investing in a Market Economy is planned to get ready understudies for an extensive variety of professions in which they will be looked with the test of assessing investment openings and settling on dynamic choices to guide money to upgrade value. Such businesses incorporate abnormal state official positions inside organizations, vocations in elective investment firms, for example, private value or bothered obligation firms, or ineffectively oversaw shared funds. An understudy moving on from this fixation ought to have the capacity to comprehend the full arrangement of crucial financial and critical powers that support or disgrace a specific investment opportunity from both a hypothetical and authentic point of view.

An issue with purchasing shares in a bear market is that notwithstanding showing up undervalued at one time, costs can at present drop alongside the market. On the other hand, an issue with not purchasing shares in a positively trending market is that regardless of showing up overvalued at one time, costs can, in any case, ascend alongside the market.

Additionally, one of the most significant reactions of cost-driven Value Investing is that an accentuation on low prices (and as of late discouraged charges) routinely deceives retail investors; in light of the fact that in a general sense low costs regularly speak to an in a general sense sound contrast (or change) in an organization's relative financial wellbeing. With that in mind, Warren Buffett has routinely stressed that "it's obviously better to purchase an awesome organization at a reasonable cost than to purchase a reasonable organization at a great cost."

Another issue is the strategy for computing the "natural value." A few experts trust that two investors can break down a similar data and achieve different conclusions concerning the inherent value of the organization and that there is no deliberate or standard approach to value a stock. A value investing system must be viewed as fruitful on the off chance that it conveys abundance returns after taking into account the risk included, where risk might be characterized in a wide range of ways, including market chance, multi-factor models or quirky risk.

Sadly, the more significant part of the "value" indexes that individuals reference, for example, the Russell 3000 Value Index, are based principally rancid off cost to book. The execution of value methodologies shifts significantly relying upon which metric you utilize. On the off chance that you picked the least expensive stocks in light of income, you did ineffectively in 2015 yet marginally over-performed throughout the most recent decade. Shares with the least expensive cost to deal proportions have done as of late.

Notwithstanding their arbitrary late execution, these measurements have their issues. We've brought up ordinarily how the cost to income proportions are characteristically imperfect and have no association with genuine value. The business number is in any event less simple for officials to control, yet it additionally overlooks auxiliary edge contrasts and the effect of the asset report.

The Solution?

Investors searching for value need to adopt an all-encompassing strategy that measures an organization's capacity to convey monetary profit to investors and evaluates the desires for future trade streams installed out its ebb and flow stock cost.

CONCLUSION

Thank you once again for downloading this book

Current accounting gauges are satisfactory for estimating structures and hardware (book value), however as our economy has moved to a more innovation/information base, a considerable lot of these scholarly resources never appear on financial proclamations.

Value investors recognize that their real investment organization is significantly more profitable as a progressing business (expected money streams, and so on.) than its benefits (market value). As a rule, it is the intangibles – licenses, trademarks, innovative work, brand, et cetera – that drives the desires of future growth, not hard resources.

In any case, you touch base at the natural or reasonable value, give yourself a room for mistakes with the possibility that if the estimation isn't right, you may overpay. If you utilize one of the administrations specified above or another source to locate the natural value, decide whether they have just considered in a wiggle room. For instance, on the off chance that you trust the inborn cost is $20 per share, give yourself an edge of wellbeing and lower the objective to $36 per share.

Numerous individuals have made fortunes utilizing a value-based way to deal with investing. This outline proposes a theory that works after some time on the off chance that you purchase precisely and hold as long as possible.

Having said that, if you enjoyed this book, then I will like to ask you for a favor, would you be kind enough to leave a review for this book? It will be greatly appreciated

Thank You and Goodluck!

www.ingramcontent.com/pod-product-compliance
Lightning Source LLC
Chambersburg PA
CBHW071125210326
41519CB00020B/6424